Piano*Trainer Series*

The Intermediate Pianist Book 1

Karen Marshall & Heather Hammond

We greatly appreciate all the feedback on the books we have received from many very gifted piano teachers. We have listened to you all! Lindsey Berwin, Barbara Bury, Andrew Dunlop, Andrew Eales, Helen Marshall, Matthew Palmer, Jo Peach, Julian Saphir, Penny Stirling, Jean White. Huge thanks also to Faber Music and Lesley Rutherford (our editor).

Dedicated to Christopher Johnson (CJ), Karen's secondary school music teacher. Your inspiring, accessible and creative teaching has been a blueprint for my own career. Huge thanks!

Answers are available on the product page on fabermusicstore.com

© 2017 by Faber Music Ltd
This edition first published in 2017
Bloomsbury House, 74–77 Great Russell Street, London WC1B 3DA
Music processed by Jackie Leigh
Text designed by Susan Clarke
Cover design by adamhaystudio.com
Printed in England by Caligraving Ltd

ISBN10: 0-571-54001-5
EAN13: 978-0-571-54001-3

To buy Faber Music publications or to find out about the full range of titles available please contact your local music retailer or Faber Music sales enquiries:
Faber Music Ltd, Burnt Mill, Elizabeth Way, Harlow CM20 2HX
Tel: +44 (0) 1279 82 89 82   Fax: +44 (0) 1279 82 89 83
sales@fabermusic.com   fabermusicstore.com

Contents

Introduction

Moving a student successfully and positively on to the intermediate levels (Grades 3 – 5) can be a tricky process. At this stage, it takes too long to learn music by rote, so **well-developed note-reading skills** are key. Students also need to have a **good understanding of style** – they can no longer simply play music the way they think it should sound to give a convincing performance. Finally, **sound technique** and **good theoretical knowledge** are required to tackle trickier repertoire. *The Intermediate Pianist* books provide a one-stop shop for building all these skills.

The material is organised into chapters that are designed to give approximately one month's work. Each chapter contains a variety of elements as described below. The music deliberately spans a range of difficulty levels, so some pieces can be learnt in just one or two weeks, whilst others are more challenging. The terms used throughout also support and reflect those required for GCSE Music.

 Quick learn

At least a grade below the ability level, these pieces and studies consolidate skills, maintain interest and improve note reading.

 Repertoire

Specially selected pieces give excellent experience of the style in each chapter.

 Technique

Exercises and activities to develop the key technical skills required.

 Challenge

Imaginative ideas to deepen musical understanding and knowledge.

 Activities

Things to do to prepare for the pieces and develop musicianship.

 Theory

A range of exercises to improve theory alongside playing ability.

 Recital pieces

Stand-alone pieces perfect for performances, unconnected to the style of the chapter.

We hope you find *The Intermediate Pianist* a journey of discovery that brings a love of music from many different periods and styles.

Happy music making!

Karen Marshall and Heather Hammond

Getting started

Activity

Included in this piece are all the styles explored in the book. Listen to your teacher play it: what do you notice about each style?

Ode to Styles

Ludwig van Beethoven
Arr. Heather Hammond

① Learning to swing

Swing rhythm is a jazz style in which the first quaver (eighth note) of each pair is slightly longer than the second:

An **offbeat** is the beat (or beats) in a bar that is less important, and not normally accented.

The **bass line** is the lowest part in a piece of music.

? Challenge

Watch a performance of the famous swing piece *Mack the Knife* by Bobby Darin. You may see him clicking on the **offbeat**. Can you click or tap along on the offbeat?

The rhythm looks like this:

⚡ Quick learn

Swinging Along

First practise playing the bass line before trying it hands together.

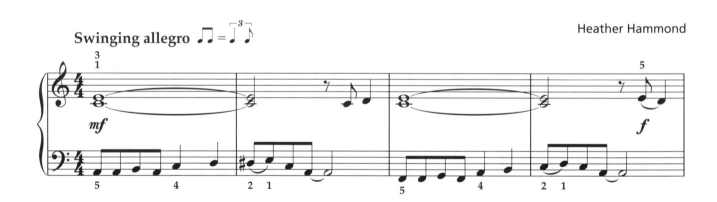

Activity  Add in some dynamic markings to this piece. Play it through first
(or your teacher could play it to you) before you decide.

Quick learn

Black Cat Swing

Heather Hammond

Know your major scales

Major and minor scales use every note name (A B C D E F G), but start on different notes. The notes of a scale move stepwise by intervals of a tone or semitone. The pattern of a major scale is:

tone   tone   semitone   tone   tone   tone   semitone.

Complete the missing notes in these major scales and arpeggios. There are no key signatures, so include any accidentals needed and any fingering you might find useful. Name each (including whether it is ascending or descending) then play it.

Name _____

Scale   Arpeggio

Name _____

Name _____

Name _____

Name _____

Bass-clef note revision

Write the name below each note to create some words:

Name the bass-clef notes, then write the same note (at the same pitch) in the treble clef.

....

....

Practise your bass-clef notes by sight-reading these four cool bass lines.

Lively bossa bass

Walking about

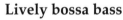

Funky moderato

Allegretto (ramble)

The Bear

This piece will help your bass-clef reading. The quavers (eighth notes) are straight, not swung.

Vladimir Rebikov

The **sustain pedal** is the pedal on the right, and is also known as the damper pedal. Find out how it works and why it is sometimes called the damper pedal.

 Technique

Kleine Studie

(Extract)

Remember to lift the pedal when the chords change, without lifting your hand off the keys at the same time. This will keep it sounding *legato*.

Robert Schumann

Describe what these terms and signs mean:

pp _____

◁ _____

Dim. e rit. _____

♩ _____
>

A tempo _____

Poco moto _____

♩ _____
=

𝄾 _____

 Activity

What can you find out about this piece by Beethoven?

The pedal marks have been left out. With your teacher's help, add them in.

Listen to the pedalling on different recordings of _Für Elise_. Then record yourself playing the piece and listen to your pedalling.

An interval is the distance between two notes. Conjunct motion is moving by step. Disjunct motion is a leap or jump. Can you find an example of a conjunct and disjunct interval in this piece?

 Repertoire

Für Elise

Ludwig van Beethoven

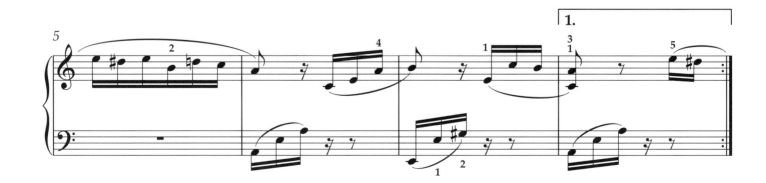

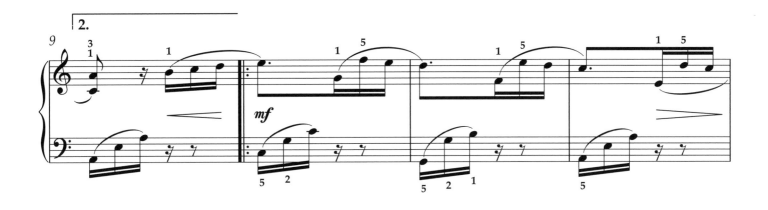

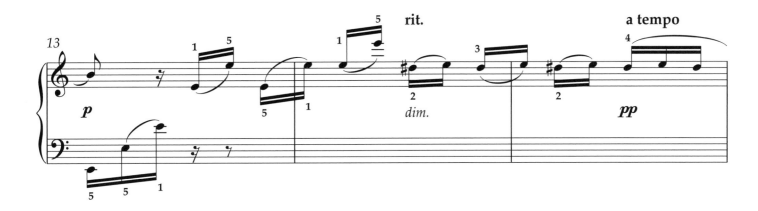

 Activity

This piece of music is in **ternary** form (the same as *Twinkle Twinkle Little Star*). This means that the first tune returns at the end, so there is an A section, a B section and then the A section again. Can you identify these sections in *Für Elise*?

3 Let's tango

A **tango** is a dance from Argentina that originated in the early 1800s. Usually written in $\frac{2}{4}$ or $\frac{4}{4}$, often with dotted rhythms, tangos are commonly in a minor key.

? Challenge

Find a video of a tango online. What do you notice about the rhythm and style of the music? Which words below best describe it?

Dramatic   Smooth   Jolting   Serious   Funny

Conjunct intervals   Disjunct intervals

⚡ Quick learn

Tango Time

Heather Hammond

Recital piece

Por una Cabeza

Carlos Gardel and Alfredo Le Pera
Arr. Heather Hammond

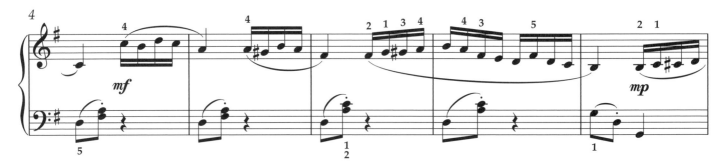

Key signatures and relative minors

Here are some common major key signatures – do you know them all?

C major	G major	F major	D major	B♭ major

Each major key has a **relative minor** which has the same key signature. You can easily work out a relative minor using the *Relative Key Song*. Start on the tonic (key note) of the major key, and sing down four semitones:

C major

You ended on an A, so the relative minor with the same key signature is A minor.

G major

You ended on an E, so the relative minor with the same key signature is _____ minor.

F major

Fill in the missing notes – what is the relative minor of F major? _____

D major

Fill in the notes for D major. The relative minor is _____

B♭ major

Fill in the notes for B♭ major. The relative minor is _____

Natural and harmonic minor scales

In **natural minor scales** you only play the notes in the key signature – there are no accidentals. So A natural minor uses the notes A B C D E F G A.

Harmonic minor scales follow the same pattern, but the seventh note is raised by a semitone. Here is A harmonic minor scale (the brackets show the semitones):

Fill in the missing notes for A harmonic minor in the left hand, then play it.

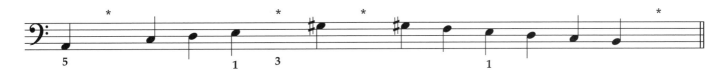

This is E harmonic minor: can you fill in the missing notes then play both scales?

This is D harmonic minor: can you fill in the missing notes then play both scales?

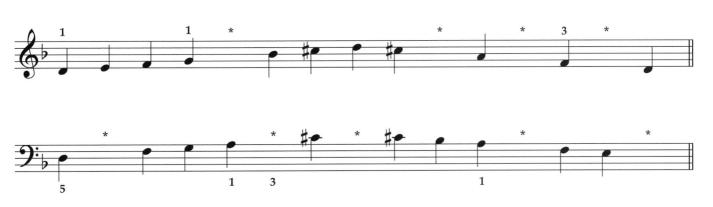

Activity   Can you identify when the piece moves from the minor to the major?

 **Recital piece**

Sorrow

From *For Children, Book 2*

Béla Bartók

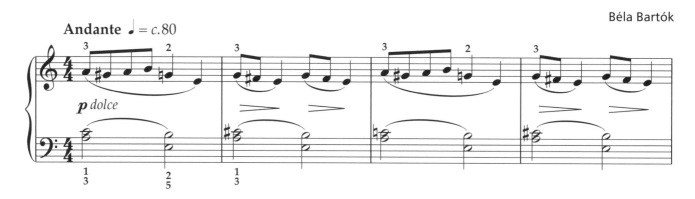

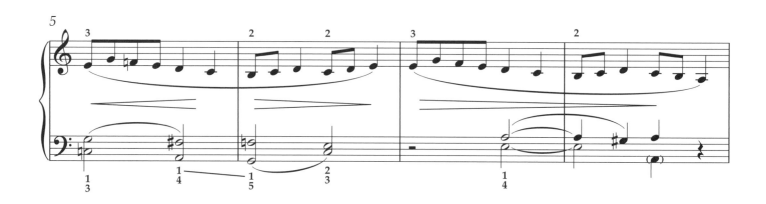

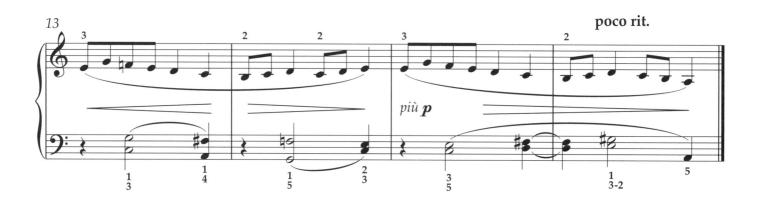

4 Exploring march style

A march is a piece of music usually in $\frac{4}{4}$, with a clear steady beat (so it can be marched to) and often with a military feel.

Challenge

Listen to a march online (perhaps find a famous one such as *Marche militaire* by Schubert). What do you notice about the rhythm and style of the music? Which words describe the music best?

Dramatic   Fast   Relentless   Soft   Slow   Energetic

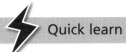

Quick learn

March of the Marionettes

Heather Hammond

Activity

Play and clap these rhythms, then write in the correct time signature for each. They are in $\frac{2}{4}$, $\frac{3}{4}$, $\frac{4}{4}$ or $\frac{6}{8}$.

 Activity

Mark the pulse as your teacher plays this by walking or clapping along.

 Repertoire

Soldiers' March

Soldatenmarsch

Robert Schumann

Introducing the circle of fifths

The circle of fifths is an image that shows all the major key signatures, along with their relative minors on the inside circle. Their order around the circle indicates the number of sharps or flats included in each key.

The circle given below has some key signature names missing – can you fill them in? Work out sharp keys by moving up a fifth each time, clockwise from the top. For the flat keys, move anti-clockwise from the top, down a fifth each time.

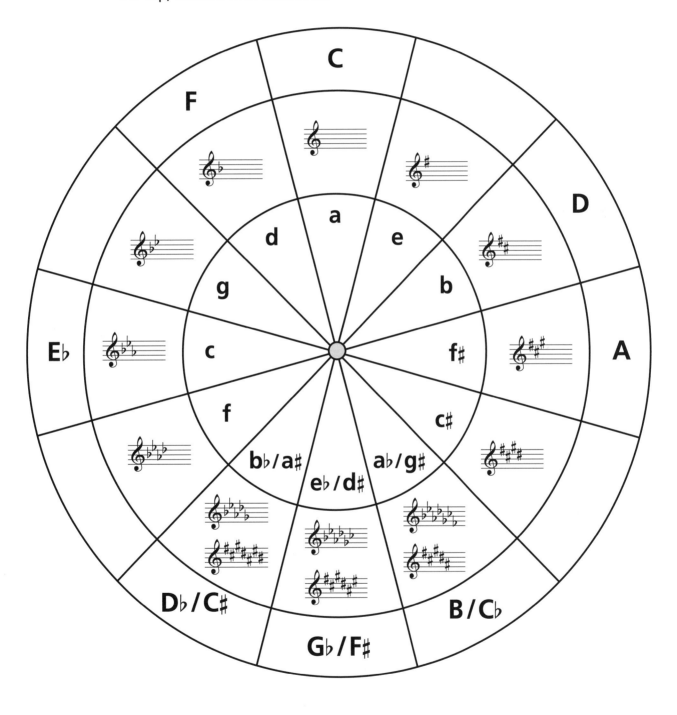

Activity

You can use this circle of fifths in your scale practice, colouring in a segment as you learn each of the scales.

Sight-read these treble-clef tunes – you may recognise some.

A **minuet** is a step dance in $\frac{3}{4}$ time that was common in the Baroque and Classical periods.

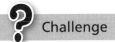

Challenge

Listen to a minuet online (perhaps find a famous one by Bach). What do you notice about the rhythm and style of the music? Which words describe it best?

Dramatic   Fast   Stately   Dance-like   In $\frac{4}{4}$ In $\frac{3}{4}$

Technique

Arpeggio exercise

These bars are adapted from a Czerny study.

Carl Czerny

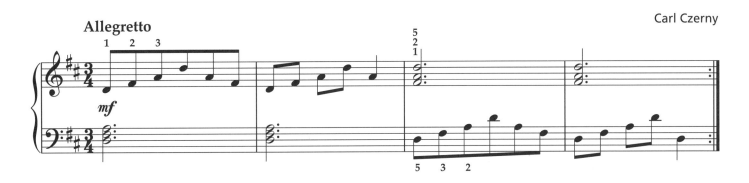

What other major keys can you play this study in? Try one from the list below.

C   G   A   E   F   B♭   E♭

Theory

Treble-clef note revision

Write the name below each note to create some words:

Activity

Baroque music was generally written without any dynamics and phrasing indications. Can you add your own to this piece? Your teacher will help you with this.

$\boldsymbol{p}$ = quiet $\boldsymbol{f}$ = loud $\boldsymbol{mf}$ = medium loud $\boldsymbol{mp}$ = medium quiet

An arpeggio uses the 1st, 3rd, 5th and 8th notes of a scale played separately. Put a bracket above or below any arpeggio patterns you can spot in the music.

Repertoire

Minuet in G

Attrib. Christian Petzold

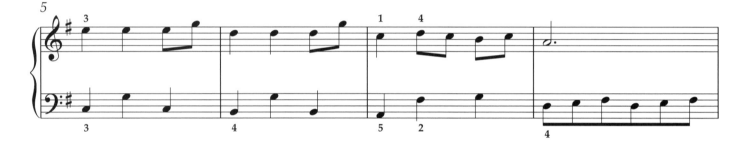

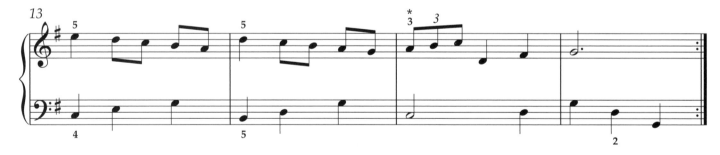

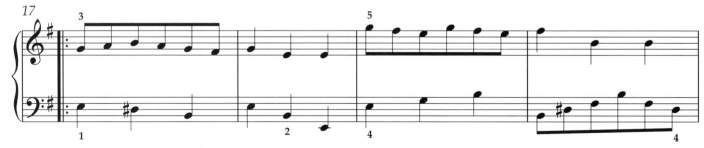

* Triplet – play 3 notes evenly in the time of a crotchet.

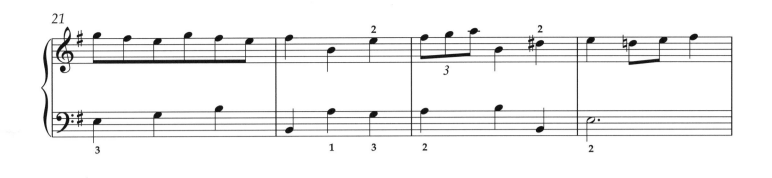

 Activity

Minuets were often included in dance suites in the Baroque period.
Find out when the Baroque period was and listen to another minuet.

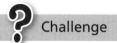

Challenge

A lullaby is sometimes called a cradle song or *berceuse* (in French). It is a gentle piece that soothes a child to sleep, usually with a rocking feel.

Listen to a lullaby online. (A popular one is *Bella's Lullaby* from the Twilight series by Carter Burwell. Try rocking to the pulse.) Which words describe it best?

Smooth   Fast   Swaying   Gentle   Dramatic   Staccato

 **Quick learn**

Lullaby

Heather Hammond and
Karen Marshall

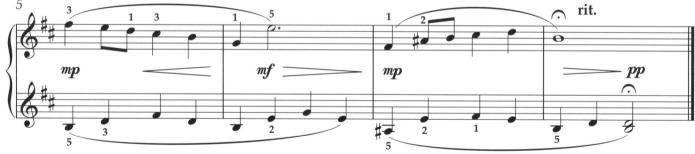

 **Activity**

Here are the words for *Hine e hine* on the next page. Think about how they might affect your performance. The music is a traditional Maori lullaby, written by a New Zealand princess.

You are crying
Little girl, little girl
You are tired
Little girl, little girl
Do not fear
For there is love
In the father's heart for you
Little girl, little girl

Hine e hine

For Katie B

Traditional Maori
Arr. Karen Marshall

How to give words a rhythm

Can you add a rhythm to the following words by Robert Louis Stevenson?

>
>   *   *   *   *   *   * *   *   (* marks the syllables)
> The **rain** is **rain** ing **all** a **round**,
>
> It falls on field and tree,
>
> It rains on the umbrellas here,
>
> And on the ships at sea.

1 Mark in the syllables; the first line has been done for you.

2 Decide on a time signature ($\frac{2}{4}$, $\frac{3}{4}$ or $\frac{4}{4}$) by marking in the strong beats. Then try tapping in 2, 3 or 4 as you say the words and see which fits best (your teacher can help you with this).

3 Then write in a note value above each syllable. Say each line and be aware of the natural rhythm of the words. You can use ♪ ♩ 𝅗𝅥 𝅗𝅥. 𝅗𝅥𝅥 Dotted rhythms can make it more interesting.

4 You can write it out on the staves below, giving the words a melody if you like. Add a tempo marking (eg. *moderato*), dynamics, phrase marks (one phrase per line of the poem) and a double bar at the end.

 **7** Playing jigs

A **jig** is a fast dance, usually in compound time ($\frac{3}{8}$, $\frac{6}{8}$, $\frac{9}{8}$ or $\frac{12}{8}$). It was popular in the Baroque period and was believed to have originated in England, Scotland and Ireland. In Italy it is called the 'giga' and in France the 'gigue'.

 Challenge

Listen to an Irish jig online – can you clap along with the pulse? Can you think of four words to describe it?

_____   _____

_____   _____

 Quick learn

Irish Jig

This melody is written for the bass clef only to give your left hand a work-out.

Traditional

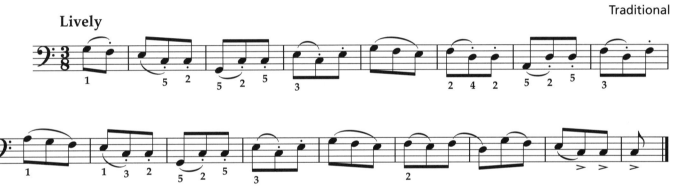

Theory

Time signatures can be either simple or compound. **Simple time signatures** have beats that can be divided in two; **compound time signatures** have beats that are divided into three. The number of beats in a time signature is also given a name: **duple** = 2 beats, **triple** = 3 beats, **quadruple** = 4 beats. So $\frac{4}{4}$ is simple quadruple. Can you draw a line to connect each time signature to its correct name?

$\frac{6}{8}$	compound triple
$\frac{3}{4}$	compound duple
$\frac{12}{8}$	simple duple
$\frac{2}{4}$	compound quadruple
$\frac{9}{8}$	simple triple

Tap the pulse as your teacher plays this gigue. Are you tapping two in a bar?

 Repertoire

Gigue a L'Angloise

Georg Philipp Telemann

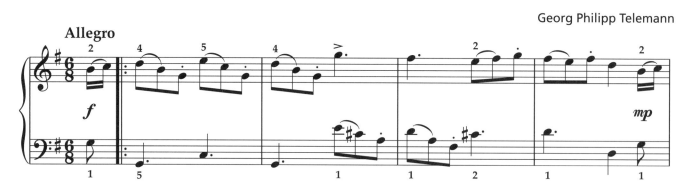

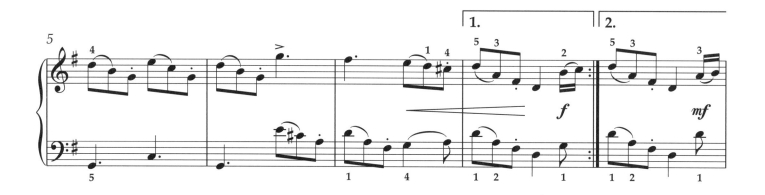

 Try these finger warm-ups from Hanon and Czerny studies.

Exercise No. 1

from *The Virtuoso Pianist Book 1*
Charles-Louis Hanon

Exercise No. 9

from *101 Exercises* Op.261
Carl Czerny

Exercise No. 10

from *101 Exercises* Op.261
Carl Czerny

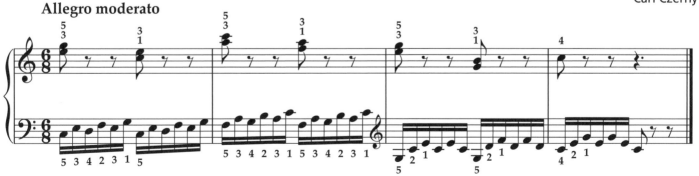

Activity   Can you find out which features of this piece are in a rock style?

 Recital piece   # Wow!

Heather Hammond

CODA

Theory

Primary triads

The primary triads in a key are the chords on the first (tonic), fourth (sub-dominant) and fifth (dominant) notes of the scale. Here are the primary triads in G major. Can you write the primary triads for C major? The first note is given for you.

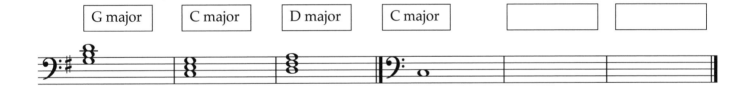

This G major scale can be harmonised using just the three primary chords. Can you work out what the missing chords could be? Write out the chords and play it.

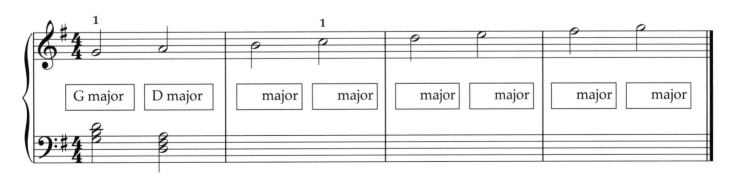

8 Let's boogie

Boogie is a style that features repetitive rhythm patterns, often with repeated chords and a swung rhythm.

 **Challenge**

Can you find a boogie piece online? You could listen to the classic *The Fives* by Hersal Thomas. What do you notice about it?

 **Activity**

Play bars 3–6 of the left-hand bass line in the piece below: this is a typical boogie bass line.

 **Quick learn**

Eager Beaver Boogie

Heather Hammond

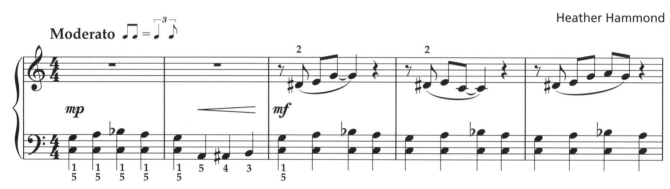

Repertoire

Bubblegum Boogie

Heather Hammond

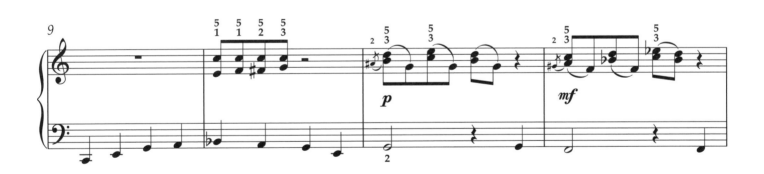

Activity

Can you identify the chords in bars 1–8 of this piece?

Recital piece

Arabesque

Friedrich Burgmüller

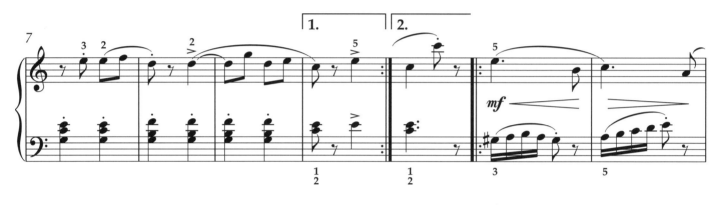

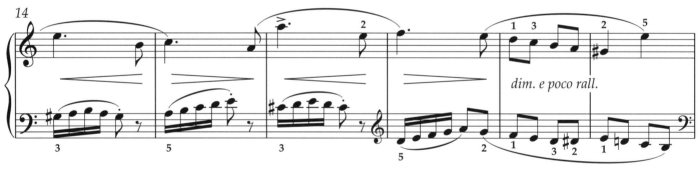

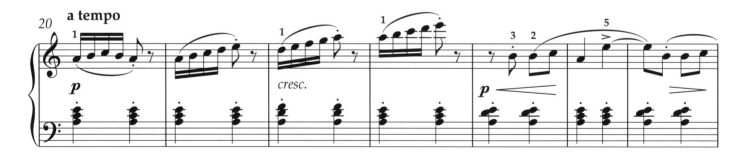

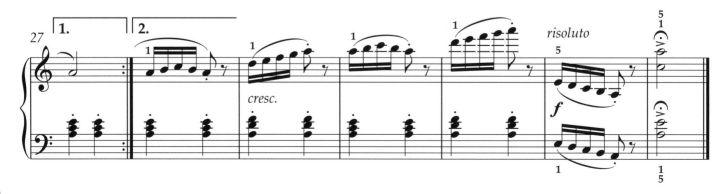

Blues is a jazzy style which is built on a chord structure called the **12-bar blues**. The characteristic sound comes from the use of the blues scale and syncopation (a rhythm which is played off the main beat(s) of the bar).

♪ Technique

Play the G blues scale in your right and left hands:

✋ Activity

Find out about the 12-bar blues chord sequence, then see if you can improvise your own right-hand blues tune. Use notes from the G blues scale above to fit over this 12-bar blues bass line.

Laid-back Blues

Laid back and bluesy

Activity   Can you hear the swung rhythms and blue notes in this piece?

Repertoire

Flying Scotsman Blues

Heather Hammond

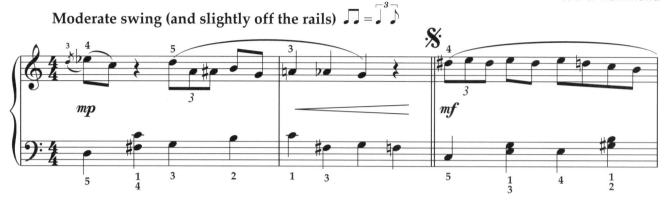

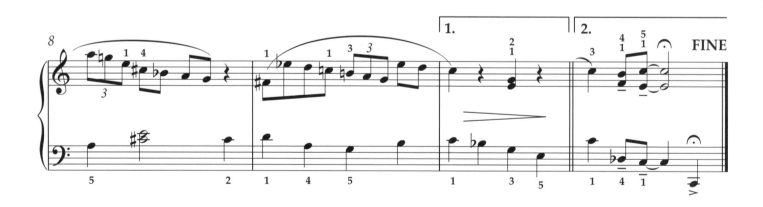

(10) Concert pieces

This section gives you a selection of pieces from different styles and periods to play now that you've completed this book. Try the activities below with every piece – you can photocopy this page if you like.

Name of piece _____

☐ Clap the pulse as your teacher plays the piece, stressing the first beat of each bar.

☐ Is it in 2, 3 or 4 time – or another time signature? _____

☐ Your teacher will play two bars from the piece – sing the melody back. (N.B. teachers can transpose the melody into singing range as needed.)

☐ Describe the style/period of the music. _____

_____

☐ What are the dynamics? _____

☐ How would you describe the tempo? (Use an Italian term if you can.)

_____

☐ Is the piece in a major or minor key (or both)? _____

☐ Your teacher will play a bar and then play it again with a change to the pitch or rhythm. What is the change?

_____

☐ Your teacher will play an interval from the piece (either a major 2nd, 3rd, perfect 4th or 5th or octave). Name the interval.

_____

☐ Circle the correct description of the time signature of the piece:

Simple duple   Compound duple
Simple triple   Compound triple
Simple quadruple   Compound quadruple

☐ Find out three facts about the composer:

_____

_____

Menuetto Op.38

(Classical)

Johann Wilhelm Hässler

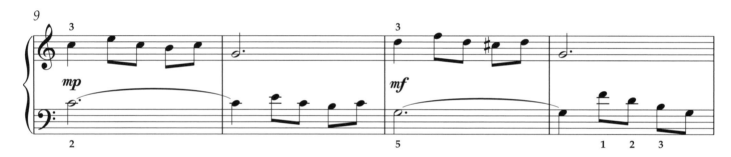

Theory

Draw a dotted minim: _____   How many counts is it worth? _____

Look at left-hand bars 1–2 and right-hand bar 8.
Which bar has a tie? _____   Which bar has a slur? _____

What do the following dynamics mean:

mp _____   *mf* _____

f _____   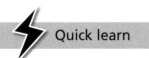 _____

Draw a crotchet rest: _____

Recital piece

The Toy
(Renaissance)

Anon.

Theory

What is the key of this piece? _____

What does a dot above or below a note mean and what is the Italian word?

_____

Draw a pause mark: _____ What does it mean? _____

Can you find an interval of a major third? Bar _____

And an interval of a perfect 5th? Bar _____

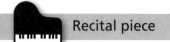
Menuetto From Sonata K.73 L.217

(Baroque)

Domenico Scarlatti

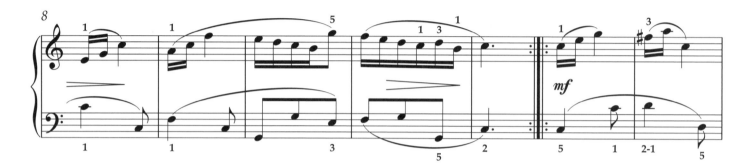

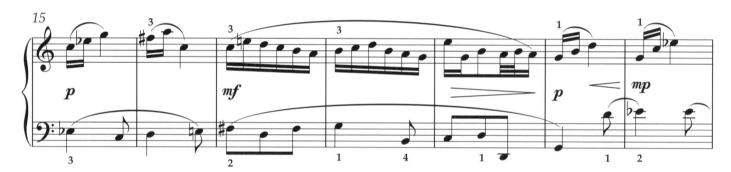

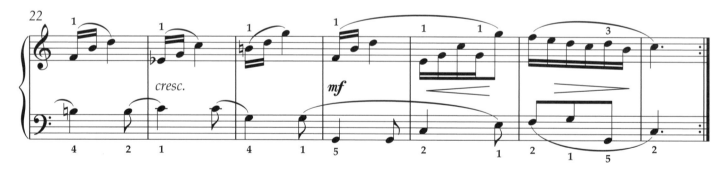

Theory

How many semiquavers (sixteenth notes) are there in a crotchet (quarter note)? _____

Can you find some demisemiquavers (thirty-second notes) in this piece? How many are in a crotchet (quarter note)? _____

Draw a repeat sign here: _____

What is a Menuetto? _____

In which bar does the music move from C major into C minor? _____

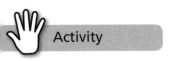

Musical styles and periods wordsearches

If you don't know what any of these words mean then look them up or ask your teacher.

The Baroque period (1600–1750)

D	C	O	N	T	R	A	P	U	N	T	A	L
B	O	U	C	R	A	B	K	B	L	O	D	S
I	L	N	F	U	G	U	E	A	W	R	A	S
T	L	I	S	G	U	T	L	C	O	N	N	A
T	E	T	C	I	U	J	V	H	I	A	C	B
A	N	N	X	G	T	U	C	S	V	M	E	D
L	R	O	S	U	H	I	K	M	M	E	S	E
R	O	C	D	E	S	A	N	G	N	N	U	R
A	T	S	H	P	J	R	N	H	W	T	I	U
C	I	S	R	G	P	E	O	D	O	S	T	G
S	R	A	F	R	D	P	C	E	E	Y	E	I
E	H	B	I	N	A	R	Y	F	B	L	S	F

1 BACH
2 SCARLATTI
3 HANDEL
4 CONTRAPUNTAL
5 DANCE SUITES
6 FIGURED BASS
7 BASS CONTINUO
8 BINARY
9 FUGUE
10 RITORNELLO
11 ORNAMENTS
12 GIGUE
13 HARPSICHORD

The Classical period (1750–1820)

Y	N	O	H	P	M	Y	S	C	G	T	A	M
I	B	H	D	F	E	R	F	E	U	B	W	R
P	E	P	I	A	N	O	D	F	D	T	C	O
S	E	N	U	T	E	M	E	H	T	E	I	A
O	T	I	C	R	S	A	T	F	G	R	Y	L
N	H	H	N	J	B	S	E	D	T	N	E	B
H	O	O	D	I	J	H	C	D	M	A	X	E
M	V	M	Y	A	R	T	N	Y	O	R	V	R
G	E	O	A	K	L	A	B	N	Z	Y	A	T
L	N	P	H	F	T	N	E	A	A	F	Z	I
J	L	H	K	E	M	O	T	M	R	O	O	B
L	W	O	U	K	S	E	T	I	T	R	W	A
K	J	N	R	V	S	T	U	C	S	M	V	S
O	I	I	N	P	R	C	N	S	B	A	R	S
M	L	C	G	S	T	N	E	M	E	V	O	M

1 HOMOPHONIC
2 THEME TUNES
3 PIANO
4 HAYDN
5 MOZART
6 BEETHOVEN
7 MINUET AND TRIO
8 TERNARY FORM
9 DYNAMICS
10 SYMPHONY
11 MOVEMENTS
12 ALBERTI BASS

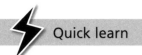 Quick learn

Song without Words

(Romantic)

Fritz Spindler

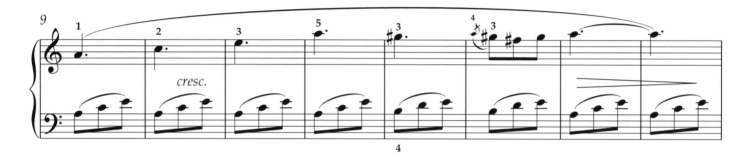

 Theory

Name a bar with all 3 notes of the tonic triad of A minor: bar _____

Find an acciaccatura. Bar _____

What does *cresc.* mean? _____

What does *poco rall.* mean? _____

Which features in the music suggest that it was written in the Romantic period?

_____

_____

Can you suggest another title for the piece? _____

Rainbow Reflections

(Contemporary)

Heather Hammond

Theory

What key is this in? _____

Explain what D.S. al Coda means. _____

_____

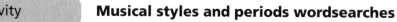

The Romantic period (1800–1900)

G	R	A	N	D	P	I	A	N	O	N	W	Y	X
Y	N	M	S	O	L	E	T	B	M	A	Y	D	C
N	A	R	E	T	R	U	D	R	P	V	T	E	H
O	T	O	X	T	P	Q	U	A	D	Z	I	F	R
M	I	N	P	E	Q	K	G	H	L	C	S	N	O
R	O	I	R	D	E	O	P	M	B	E	O	N	M
A	N	P	E	R	R	H	J	S	I	N	U	A	A
H	A	O	S	H	U	I	H	D	F	Y	T	M	T
H	L	H	S	Y	T	S	O	G	H	J	R	U	I
C	I	C	I	T	X	L	I	U	L	X	I	H	C
I	S	W	O	H	E	T	L	K	G	M	V	C	D
R	M	V	N	M	T	R	I	P	L	E	T	S	E

1 EXPRESSION
2 TEXTURE
3 PEDAL
4 MELODIES
5 VIRTUOSITY
6 CHOPIN
7 BRAHMS
8 SCHUMANN
9 NATIONALISM
10 GRAND PIANO
11 CHROMATIC
12 DOTTED RHYTHM
13 TRIPLETS
14 RICH HARMONY

The Contemporary period (1900–present day)

Z	V	N	A	T	R	H	M	L	P	U	O	P	R
B	V	W	T	N	V	A	T	H	O	I	T	C	M
R	A	O	S	T	O	P	S	D	L	N	S	I	E
S	U	C	E	B	H	S	L	E	Y	D	P	T	L
M	G	D	K	O	T	R	A	B	T	R	S	S	O
H	H	N	H	B	C	F	V	U	O	O	E	I	D
T	A	X	M	D	A	R	R	S	N	S	V	N	Y
Y	N	B	I	W	I	T	E	S	A	Y	E	O	F
H	W	A	N	L	V	Q	T	Y	L	N	N	I	R
R	I	D	I	S	S	O	N	A	N	C	E	S	A
Y	L	R	M	T	L	P	I	D	Z	O	A	S	G
L	L	A	A	I	Y	O	E	N	L	P	T	E	M
O	I	M	L	K	M	M	G	P	Y	A	O	R	E
P	A	L	I	N	E	L	R	N	J	T	N	P	N
G	M	P	S	J	L	Y	A	K	A	E	A	M	T
J	S	H	T	O	I	U	L	K	W	D	L	I	S

1 DEBUSSY
2 BARTOK
3 VAUGHAN WILLIAMS
4 POLYRHYTHMS
5 MINIMALIST
6 IMPRESSIONISTIC
7 DISSONANCES
8 POLYTONAL
9 MELODY FRAGMENTS
10 SPIKY
11 LARGE INTERVALS
12 ATONAL
13 SYNOCOPATED

Sam's Jam

(Jazz)

Heather Hammond

Theory

Are the quavers (eighth notes) straight or swung? _____

Describe the dynamics and articulation. _____

Are the phrases long, short or a mixture? _____

Musical style wordsearch

Jazz style

D	R	A	D	N	A	T	S	Z	Z	A	J	N	W
A	K	J	U	E	I	G	O	O	B	V	Y	V	S
B	L	M	K	I	T	U	I	H	A	S	G	C	C
S	N	A	E	L	R	O	W	E	N	E	P	U	O
M	I	L	E	S	D	A	V	I	S	U	F	S	T
S	E	U	L	B	R	A	B	E	V	L	E	W	T
N	R	D	L	F	E	E	T	S	E	B	R	S	J
P	O	E	I	D	G	M	H	G	O	R	P	T	O
S	Y	C	N	C	J	I	M	V	N	E	K	X	P
F	E	R	G	L	N	T	S	N	A	I	O	P	L
G	L	D	T	K	H	G	C	U	D	V	W	Z	I
H	Z	N	O	I	T	A	P	O	C	N	Y	S	N
I	A	J	N	M	D	R	O	H	C	Z	Z	A	J

1 DUKE ELLINGTON
2 MILES DAVIS
3 SCOTT JOPLIN
4 JAZZ STANDARD
5 BOOGIE
6 BLUES
7 SWING
8 TWELVE BAR BLUES
9 RAGTIME
10 MODES
11 SYNCOPATION
12 JAZZ CHORD
13 NEW ORLEANS

 Activity

Revision quiz Link each style of piece to the correct description.

Tango	A Baroque dance usually in compound time
March	A stately dance in three time
Minuet	A piece of music with a military feel
Lullaby	A dance from Argentina, often with dotted rhythms and in a minor key
Jig / gigue	A rocking melody written for soothing a baby